Hope for the Rejected Woman

*Loak what the 'Lord' has done
with a broken life*

Mary Cunnane

Joel 2:25

Hope for the Rejected Woman

Mary Cunnane

Companion Press
P.O. Box 310
Shippensburg, PA 17257-0310

"Good Stewards of the
Manifold Grace of God"

ISBN 1-56043-526-7

For Worldwide Distribution
Printed in the U.S.A.

Dedication

I dedicate this book to my late brother "John Carney" who shared my life. He lived to see me come through my life of rejection victoriously. He was looking forward to this publication as he encouraged me to use my writing skills. I praise God for blessing me with a lovely brother for 60 long years.

Recommendations for this book

Incredible! what God can do with a broken life. Mary reminds us of how our tears, sufferings and trials can be used as a way to the cross, in which to be joined to Christ.

She demonstrates a clear path to a trusting heart which feels real heartbreak and loss, yet praises God in all things.

When father and mother forsake me, the Lord will take me up. The life of Mary Cunnane in Hope for the Rejected Woman is a living testimony of God's faithfulness to those who have been disappointed in life's journey.

Paul and Nuala O'Higgins

As the pastor of Good News Church, which Mary Cunnane attends, I joyfully recommend this book to you. After 20 years in the trenches of pastoring local churches, I enthusiastically embrace every new, biblically based, spiritempowered tool for setting people free. The sacrifice of Christ on the cross is perfect and those who, like Mary Cunnane, have applied its power, see tremendous results. May I encourage you to ingest both the scripture and the personal testimony which Mary offers and look to Heaven for your own healing. May God bless you and heal you and turn you into an agent of healing like Mary Cunnane!

Geoffrey Buck

In Second Corinthians 3:18 we read that "we" who with unveiled faces all reflect the Lord's glory are being transformed into His likeness (NIV). Thank you, Mary for pulling back the veil and letting us see Jesus' transforming power in your crises. What the devil meant for evil, God meant it for good.

Ruth May

Dear Mom:

Suffering can cripple our emotions. I admire your courage and strength. Only God could turn your life around. I know your story will heal many other broken women.

Your son,
Anthony

"Beauty for ashes" is the only way I can describe Mary. The quality that makes her an inspiration to thousands of rejected women is her humility. Nowhere in this book has she taken any credit for her victory, but has given her Savior all the glory.

Mary Regan

Jeremiah 29:11 (NIV)

"For I know the plans I have for you," declares the Lord, "plans to prosper you and not to harm you, plans to give you hope and a future."

Contents

Foreword xi
Introduction xiii

Chapter		Page
1	The Tragic News	1
2	My Divorce Decree	7
3	The Dispose Summons that Evicted Me Out of My House Forever	13
4	God Is in the Business of New Beginnings	23
5	My First Christmas Alone with Jesus .	33
6	My Family Unit	41
7	Another Blow: Without Medical Insurance	47
8	My Journey Across America	51

Chapter		Page
9	How I Found the Holy Spirit	63
10	My Loveless Life as a Child	69
11	Sharing My Testimony	77
12	My Seven Years with Ruth Sweeney	83
13	God Multiplied My Loss into Something Greater: Financially, Spiritually, Physically and Emotionally	87
14	God Did Not Show Me the Victory Till I Knew It Was Him	95
15	My Lovely Brother John Was Called Home to the Lord	101

Foreword

Every woman who reads this book will be strengthened in some way by the journey of faith that Mary Cunnane records in *Hope for the Rejected Woman*. Many women in America today face similar trials because the home and the family are so under attack.

Through Christ, Mary Cunnane has overcome in spite of all obstacles. Additionally, she has lifted up the banner of hope to others to inspire them to not look back as did Lot's wife in Genesis 19:26. She encourages us to go forward in new strength, trusting God to work everything together for the good. This remarkable book will encourage everyone and especially those who suffer through the agony of a broken marriage and the resulting rejection and hurt.

Mary's life is a testimony of God's healing power for the whole person. Each of us, at one time or another and in one way or the other, faces the hurt of rejection. This book will help take you across the waters of difficulty into the safe port of Christ's abiding arms. Truly He is the Prince of Peace who is nigh unto them who are of a broken and contrite spirit. Mary's life is truly a witness to people everywhere.

Sincerely in Christ,
Nora Lam

Introduction

Everyone's life is a story. Everyone's life could be a book, a movie, a TV series or even a bestseller paperback. For many years I have read testimonies of great men and women. I had dreamed of being the author of one, but I thought I had to be rich and famous, graduate with a college degree, have the right tools, come from the right background or be the right celebrity.

Although I did not have any of these qualifications, I never lost sight of the desire to be an author. Now God has finally opened the door for me to write my own testimony, not just to fulfill a lifelong dream or to prove myself a heroine for surviving the pain of a deep emotional crisis in my life, but to give Him all the honor and glory for restoring this broken vessel; for repairing all the pieces of broken pottery in my life, healing that wounded spirit within me; for setting me free of the bondage of rejection and for making me the person He intended me to be.

Today we live in a world of drugs, abortion, alcohol, lust, pornography and gambling. Praise God I never had any of these addictions, even though I was the product of a broken home from my childhood and from my marriage. When you read my story you will probably wonder how I ever had the courage to dream or become victorious. But you see, by ourselves we are worthless, but with God all things are possible (Matt. 19:26). If I had not trusted God with my broken life, I would have crumbled.

I went through an experience that was one of the cruelest and most emotional crises any human being could endure. I know the heartache of that time. I know what it is like to be rejected, wounded, devastated and alone in the dry desert, wondering if one will ever recover and start over. I know what it is to fail just about as miserably as any woman can fail; I've been there. Only a miracle from God could ever set me *free* and redeem me from my pit of destruction.

I believe God has a plan for all of our lives if we follow Him, walk in His path and trust and dedicate our lives to Him. After I made this decision, *old things passed away and all things became new* (II Cor. 5:17).

No matter what setback you may be experiencing, *you can recover*. I never put God on a shelf, no matter how bad the circumstances were, no matter how many times I got hurt, struck down or shattered to pieces. God always picked me up. He specializes in mending broken hearts and in making something beautiful of our lives. What He did for me He can do for you. God is bigger than any problem we ever have. He is bigger than any need we are facing. No matter how big that giant of despair, discouragement, fear, disease or strife in family relationships is, He can turn it around.

When I lost my marriage, my children and my home and found myself alone on the highway of life, what I thought was the end became the beginning of an abundant life in the Holy Spirit.

In every trial, crisis and adversity, there is a seed of equal benefit. If you look for that seed and plant it, God will multiply it into something greater than the loss you experienced.

When I read the Book of Job, I learned that he also lost everything: his possessions, his health and his family. His children were killed in an accident, his business went under, his health failed and he could not work any more. His close friends blamed him for all those problems. I have often heard it said that everybody either has a problem, lives with a problem or is a problem. But Job planted a seed of forgiveness and prayer for the enemies who tried to destroy him. As a result, he reaped a harvest of full restoration: twice what he owned before, healing to perfect health and a new family. (See Job 42:8-17.)

As I meditated on Job's restoration story, I discovered that *forgiveness* was the key that unlocked my giant of despair and set me free.

I had the faith and the determination that God would not only help me weather the pain of rejection, but that in His time He would fit all my suffering into a purposeful plan to be used for His glory in the healing of other rejected women. I realized then that this book could not be written for personal gain or recognition, as it could not minister to anyone till God's purpose for it was fulfilled through *the power of foriveness.*

Four years ago God opened the door for me to share my testimony in international women's Fellowship meetings across America, Canada and the Caribbean islands. Many hurting, wounded women were emotionally healed and restored from similar crises in their lives. Many of them have asked me for my testimony, which is too long to record it all on a tape. Their request confirms God's timing is right for the birth of this book which I wrote to help and to contribute healing to all hurting women who have suffered the pain of rejection. As you read of God's provision in my life, you too will find new hope as you discover that there is *Hope for the Rejected Woman.*

As God plants the seed of greatness within you, you will find a new purpose for your life and you will walk in a new awareness of the authority you have in your Creator. You will experience a new depth of love and commitment as God's love flows through you in a greater dimension. You will receive a new revelation of all the things God has prepared for you as you journey through my healing story.

Chapter 1

The Tragic News

Hebrews 13:6

So that we may boldly say, The Lord is my helper, and I will not fear what man shall do unto me.

It was a cold November morning, the eve of Thanksgiving '77. I was awakened by my doorbell. Then the voice of a young man from the Queens County Courthouse, New York, asked if Mary Cunnane lived here. "Yes," I replied, "that's me."

"I have a summons for you, sign here."

As I was signing, I was muttering, "I don't remember getting a parking violation I did not take care of." He abruptly and hurriedly answered me, "It's not a parking summons, it's your divorce papers."

Before I had time to question where he got them, he was gone, never even wishing me a "Happy Thanksgiving."

I walked upstairs holding the document which contained the tragic news that my marriage was being dissolved by divorce. Sobbing, I knelt by my bed. Looking up at the cross, I cried out to the Lord to help me accept it and endure the pain that was already penetrating my being, the shock was so devastating.

In that moment of despair, the flashbacks of my life of rejection and past hurts started to haunt me. Years of pain and suffering erupted and attacked me in an invasion of my mind and spirit. Yes, I was shattered and broken in pieces. It was the most painful, emotional, draining experience and it was accompanied by the doubt of ever recovering. It was a pain that no pill or prescription could heal.

I realize now that was satan's plan of destruction for my life, as I've since discovered in John 10:10 that satan comes "to steal, and to kill, and to destroy." My honesty was rewarded with a clear conscience. It was so clear that I knew in my heart this crisis was not of God, even though Tony and I weathered some difficult times together.

One of satan's favorite tactics is to put a permanent guilt trip on you by allowing you to dwell on your past failures. That does not reap any benefit at all, but instead brings a mountain of pain, causing you to believe that you can never recover and start over.

Paul reminds us in Philippians 3:13 to throw off the chains of the past and take up our victory, "forgetting those things which are behind, and reaching forth unto those things which are before." Unless we are willing to let go of all the hurts, failures, grudges, fears, critical attitudes and problems that developed as a result of the events that led up to this crisis, we will be chained to the past.

Divorce is something we hear happening in other people's lives: in soap operas, in the lives of celebrities, etc. We would rather believe it happened only in movies or books. But the Bible teaches us that we all will let each other down. Even the most beautiful rose has thorns. Most couples find it impossible to continue living in a loving relationship because they omit the third strand of the cord that binds them together. It takes three to make a marriage; you cannot leave God out.

Divorce was the last thing I expected to hit my life. I thought love was a fruit that was always in season. In the society where I lived, in New York in the 70's, divorce became an epidemic. Even the Catholic Church accepted it and allowed remarriage through the process of an annulment, which is not biblical. Turmoil seemed to have prevailed and it hit many broken homes. God hates divorce; He views it as sin, as a breaking of His covenant laws in a union that He Himself instituted.

Satan attacked my marriage during a business venture in Ireland in the 60's. After we returned to New York in 1970, he kept gnawing at it till he ripped it asunder. Shortly afterwards I had two close cousins who suffered divorce, followed by a string of friends. I was no longer a lonely victim of the crisis of divorce, but neither did I ever entertain loneliness.

Being alone is not a time of loneliness or grief, it is a time of becoming. It is not what happens to us in life that matters, it's how we react or what we do with it. How we handle our lives can influence others and change their destinies.

During times of crises, life around us changes quickly. For me, people who were lifetime friends and family hibernated to their closets like I was no longer part of them, or like divorce was a contagious disease that contaminated our relationship. Unlike Lot's wife, who looked back and became a pillar of salt, I chose to burn my bridges behind me. I could have allowed the death of my marriage to paralyze my emotional being and restrict it to a life of wilderness and isolation, but I chose to make it a pathway to a new life in Christ.

It is He who has transformed my life into a healing process for all wounded women who suffered the hurricane of divorce and who have struggled in the hopeless fight for survival. Why allow the actions of someone else to destroy your life? Why permit the acts of another to drag you down and rob you of your peace and joy when you have the freedom to choose your own source of happiness? Philippians 2:13 says, "For it is God which worketh in you both to will and to do of His good pleasure." The greatest of all sin is *not* believing that God has the power to deliver and to protect us from being destroyed.

Would He purposely ask us to take up crosses that He knows will sap all our human energies and leave us lying helpless, even to the point of giving up?

Women become emotional cripples by leaning on their husbands for their happiness and by living for years under this influence, even after they have convinced themselves they have a right to happiness. But they believe their husbands have a right to create it for them. Then, when tragedy hits, they are suddenly helpless. Their lives seem unproductive, like a dirty waste lot where no seed can grow. Self-doubt and people's "put-downs" cause the spirit of depression to take root in these women.

The pain and torture of divorce prevents women from walking in victory. Women are not second class citizens. God created men and women equal and in His image. We must discover the rights and privileges of our divine citizenship. We must experience the spiritual medication that can rejuvenate our lives.

Our mental attitude is the key factor in determining the outcome of the circumstances. It will produce either life...or death.

Our heart's attitude determines our spiritual attitude. We must learn to walk above the circumstances and turn satan's attacks into opportunities for a blessing. God wants each of us to live a life of stability under His protection. For me, He had already made provision for the fear that erupted in me. He saw my problem as an opportunity to work a miracle in me.

I had to acknowledge that miraculous power in my weakness, to give me strength and courage for the battle ahead.

Isaiah 41:10 (AMP)

Fear not; [there is nothing to fear] for I am with you; do not look around you in terror and be dismayed, for I am your God, I will strengthen and harden you [to difficulties]; yes, I will help you; yes, I will hold you up and retain you with My victorious right hand of rightness and justice.

Chapter 2

My Divorce Decree

Isaiah 54:17a

No weapon that is formed against thee shall prosper; and every tongue that shall rise against thee in judgment thou shalt condemn.

Most women come out of a divorce decree financially secure with alimony, a furnished house, insurance, hospitalization and a share of their life's savings, but all these benefits were denied me. It was another devastating moment of despair when the judge read the decision, for not only did I lose all financial benefits, I also lost custody of my son and the possession of our marital home.

No one, only God knows, why such an injustice happened to an honest citizen of the land where equal rights and justice prevail for female citizens.

I was defeated by being honest. I never had a bank book in my own name; everything I had was jointly owned because I always felt that was God's divine plan for the marriage unit.

After we lost our life's savings in our business venture in Ireland, we had a humble beginning in starting over again in an apartment in New York. For the first time since I retired to raise our three children, I was able to go back to work as a waitress. Things had changed financially in that field. In a few years I was able to save $20,000, which I used to put a down payment on our marital house. Naturally I put both names on the mortgage, never thinking that five years down the road a judge would disbelieve my honesty and have me thrown out of my house. Because the down payment came out of a joint account, I had no proof for the judge that it was my investment, but God sees our hearts and He declared in His Word that no weapon formed against us shall prosper and that every false judgment shall be condemned (Isa. 54:17). We can fool man most of the time, but we can never fool God.

Divorce was very new to New York state in the 70's and equal distribution was not yet legalized.

Whoever got custody, got possession of the marital dwelling. Since our two daughters were over 18, our 15-year-old son was the only infant issue. His custody was awarded to his father and I was given 60 days to leave my home. No one, only satan, could preordain this injustice and use innocent people to plot destruction in my life.

I realize now that the decision made in the court that day was not God's choice. It was not Tony's plan. It was a demonic force of the enemy who is in the business of destroying marriages and breaking up the family unit.

Where was God through all this? He allowed it to happen so He could work His plan and purpose by proving His power and glory through my distress. He knew how to get my attention. Divorce is a major surgery. With a physical affliction, a wise doctor will try to treat the affliction with methods less drastic. So it is with divorce. It is a last resort alternative. But by God's grace there can be life after divorce.

Since I did not have a close relationship with the Lord then like I do today, I was struggling with this terrible injustice that had betrayed me. Fear, which is the product of ignorance, gripped me. I was scared of the unknown.

At the time, I was depending on my lawyer to create a miracle and change the decree of the decision. This dependency is the parallel to the condition in the lives of most victims today when they put their faith in man. *Faith is a fact* but *faith is also an act*!

Let's look at the biblical story of Isaac's two sons, Jacob and Esau. Jacob deceived his brother Esau by extorting the firstborn's birthright. Not stopping there, Jacob also deceived his father Isaac into giving him the blessing that, by tradition, should have gone to his older brother. Esau, feeling as cheated as I did when I struggled with that terrible injustice, reacted and vowed to kill his brother.

Jacob fled into Haran, a far-off land, for 21 years. During that time God did spiritual surgery on Esau's heart and erased the revenge that his brother feared, so they could forgive and be reconciled. God also blessed Esau abundantly with more than he ever had before his crisis. God also blessed Jacob, and the brothers were united in peace and love. (See Genesis 25-33.)

We run and cry and whimper when tragedy hits us, not knowing that all the time we have power and authority with our Savior if we would turn to Him and receive Him into our lives.

John 1:12

> *But as many as received Him, to them gave He power to become the sons of God, even to them that believe on His name.*

Chapter 3

The Dispose Summons that Evicted Me Out of My House Forever

Psalm 40:2

He brought me up also out of an horrible pit, out of the miry clay, and set my feet upon a rock, and established my goings.

I was crushed, bruised and emotionally crippled with the thought of being evicted from my house permanently and of facing a new life alone after 21 years of marriage. It is one thing to lose your marriage, but to lose your children and your home? How does a family break apart and become like strangers? How does it begin to crumble? This was my family, the husband and children whom I loved and with whom I shared my life. Now they are ready to throw me out like a garbage bag full of broken pottery.

I had a lot of soul-searching to do, a lot of decisions to make, as I struggled with the spirit of rejection. My family and friends all got lost in their closets, as if they rejoiced at my failure. I was caught with no place to go for resource, no court to plead my case, nothing left to do but turn to God, which was my best source of supply. God did not promise us a parade of roses into the Kingdom. But He did promise us an escape. Once we experience the truth, it's hard not to see it. Once we see God's sovereignty, it's hard to claim autonomy.

It was hard for me not to nourish a root of bitterness. I could not deny the reality of the injustice done to me. Here I stand with a broken rope in my hand, and what do I do with the pain? It was hard for me to understand that God loved me and ordained the events of my life.

Job had gone through a wrenching time in his life as well. Every rope that ever held him together had broken, and he knew God more deeply than I did. The bitterness he spoke was cutting.

Since I could not be honest about my failure and accept my trial of injustice (as we live in a fallen world), the issue looked like defeat, but somehow I felt that victory was on the way.

For eight months after the divorce was finalized I lived in the house with my family. It was like living with a group of strangers, and I wondered how we became strangers. Only the enemy could have moved in and destroyed what our friends thought was a model family.

I also rebelled as I reflected on my hard labor, saving my waitress tips for two years to buy this house, and the unspeakable joy that overwhelmed me as I reached my goal. Now my joy was shattered. I had to legally leave the house and never return to it again without permission. I could see this happening only to an adulteress, an alcoholic or a drug addict.

During this waiting period, satan attacked my physical body. I was admitted to the hospital for major surgery for a bleeding tumor in my colon. After three weeks of testing in the hospital, the doctors decided the tumor was behind my small bowel and could be reached only by removing the bowel. It was another demonic attack. I was petrified with fear that I would break down, collapse and never make it.

Psalm 9:9 (AMP)

*The Lord also will be a refuge and a high
tower for the oppressed, a refuge and a stronghold in times of trouble....*

It was another season of suffering. Tears flowed
onto my pillow as I laid on my bed of affliction,
awaiting major surgery. Feeling totally defeated
after losing all that I held dear, it was now another
blow to have to face my new life without my bowel.
Satan was having a real heyday making hash of
my life.

Philicia, a Christian lady I worked with, called
me when she heard of my surgery to ask if she
could pray for my healing. It was like a voice from
Heaven saying, "Help is on the way; hang on." She
started to pray on the phone in her heavenly language. It was the first time I heard someone praying in tongues, but I did not question it. I was so
desperate for help that I accepted it in faith. God
knew it was the perfect time to introduce it to me.
He had been waiting for 48 years to get my attention.

I faced surgery very bravely the next morning.
On the operating table I asked the Lord to take my
life if I had cancer and no bowel. After all, what
had I left to live for?

Hours later I woke up in the recovery room lis-
tening to my surgeon's voice saying, "Mary, there

was no cancer and we did not take out your bowel. We could not find what we saw in the X-rays." When I got back to my room that evening, Philicia, the lady with the gift of healing, called to see how I was. I told her the good news and she said, "I know. I had you listed on all the prayer groups and we claimed your healing. Don't you know there is Someone who cares for you? His name is Jesus."

None of my family members visited me in the hospital, which was no help to my healing process. When I got home, none had any welcome for me, but kept looking to see if I had any signs of packing and moving out of their lives.

The next few weeks of recuperation were crucial, wondering if I'd ever recover physically or emotionally or even make it into my new life.

Finally more tragic news came, this time to my bedroom door. Tony had filed a dispose summons to evict me out of my house. At about 11 p.m. one night, I was getting ready for bed when two policemen knocked on my bedroom door. Holding a bunch of documents in his hand, one of them said, "Mrs. Cunnane, you are under arrest".

With tear-filled eyes I said, "What did I do wrong?"

"You are trespassing! You are not supposed to be here as of such a date." Holding the handcuffs in his hand, the other one said, "We will take you to jail tonight, and you will have to face trial tomorrow."

Trembling with fear and sobbing, I asked to make a phone call. While I was on the phone, the Lord dealt with their hearts. When I finished, they gave me an alternative: to leave voluntarily right away and never return without permission, or spend the night in jail. If I went to jail, I would be convicted of a crime and it would be recorded for life on my records, even though I had no knowledge of committing a crime.

The police wanted to take me to a woman's shelter for the night, but that sounded weird. Yet it was better than jail. I knew there was no point in phoning my relatives and friends who lived nearby as their doors and their stony hearts were now closed to me. Still, I would try calling others first.

Psalm 118:5-7

I called upon the Lord in distress: the Lord answered me, and set me in a large place. The Lord is on my side; I will not fear: what can man do unto me? The Lord taketh my part with them that help me: therefore shall I see my desire upon them that hate me.

At midnight I was still ringing people's phones from a public phone booth, looking for shelter for the night. When I could not get anyone to answer, I thought, "I should have gone with the policemen to the women's shelter; it's better than sleeping in my car." Finally Mary Austin, a friend who lived in the area, answered my call and invited me to spend the night with her.

Next morning when I knew the house was empty, Mary and I went in to get my clothes. That was a big risk after the police told me I would get six months in jail if I went in without permission. But when satan closed my home's door on me, I knew God would open another. The enemy rejoiced when he saw my family throw me out like a bag of garbage, but my disappointment become God's appointment.

I relate to Joseph when I read his story in Genesis (37-47). He was one of Jacob's 12 sons, and his father's favorite. Joseph was very sensitive to the things of God. God spoke to him in dreams. When he shared one of his dreams with his brothers, that all of them had fallen down and paid homage to him, they felt it was a very real threat. When their jealousy turned to rage, they were ready to kill him.

One day Joseph came to the fields with a message and some provisions from his father. The older brothers plotted to get rid of Joseph and cut him out of their family dwelling. As a result, they sold him into slavery to the Ishmeelites for 20 pieces of silver. The traders then took Joseph into Egypt. His brothers thought he would never be heard of again, but God had a purpose for him.

Joseph was alone in a world of slavery, but God met his every need and kept blessing him. Again tragedy overtook him: he was unjustly accused by his master's wife. This injustice committed him to prison, but he continued to serve God and He blessed him. Finally Joseph was placed in charge of the other prisoners and, in that role, he befriended Pharaoh's baker and butler, who had lost favor with Pharaoh. Joseph was able to interpret their dreams.

Later, when the butler was restored to his former position, Pharaoh had a dream that troubled him greatly. None of his wisest counselors could interpret it for him. The butler remembered Joseph and his special gifts. So one day, after years of discouragement, slavery and hardship, Joseph went from being prisoner to being Prime Minister of all Egypt. His interpretation of a dream in prison had been a seed that reaped a harvest beyond his youthful mistake of telling his first dreams. In his new position, he was able to provide for his father Jacob and his brothers in a time of severe famine.

The seed Joseph had planted for an equal benefit blotted out the power of the past tragedies in his life.

I relate to this story, especially when in the next few chapters I share with you how God blessed me and gifted me on my road to recovery. For instance, I was never alone. God was always with me like He was with Joseph.

I am sure many of you have a Joseph story in your life. But if you cannot handle suffering, trials and rejection, you cannot be used of God. He can use only a broken, rejected life to demonstrate His power. His ultimate purpose is for you to be victorious in *Him*.

Chapter 4

God Is in the Business of New Beginnings

Psalm 34:19

Many are the afflictions of the righteous: but the Lord delivereth him out of them all.

It was a beautiful fall day in September '78 when I set out to drive to Florida in search of a new life, still feeling devastated and wounded. I drove by my house to take a last look at my pit of destruction. I could not live close by, especially among my loved ones who rejected me and dumped me out like a bag of garbage. It was better to move out of the state and begin a new life elsewhere.

I secured employment in Florida before I left, so at least I had a destination, even though it was temporary. It was a thousand-mile drive, and I did not have any experience with long-distance highway driving. I had a driver's license in my wallet for 17 years, but Tony had decided I did not know how to drive and after awhile I believed him. It was always his car, not ours. I kept the license validated in hopes that someday God would bless me with a car and the gift of driving.

Philippians 4:13

I can do all things through Christ which strengtheneth me.

He not only blessed me with the gift of driving, He also gave me the courage to drive coast to coast and all through the lower 48 states. He even gifted me with two new cars, which I will share later in my story.

On my journey I stopped in Silver Springs, Maryland, to visit some very precious Irish friends, Bridie and Buddy Howes. They hosted me for quite a restful weekend. They were the first people to show me love on my road to recovery.

New York was far behind me now, and I was faced with the reality that I must stand alone. I could have easily built a shrine around my hurts and spent the rest of my life worshiping at it, but I decided not to be a tenant of the past. Besides, the worldly goods and possessions I had spent years accumulating had evaporated overnight. It was just my car and me now. The trunk of my car contained only my clothing. So I decided not to carry any excess baggage from the past, or I would keep rehashing it into my new-found life.

Yes, it was hard to begin again. It was so easy to give up hope in a world without love. I knew I could be permanently destroyed beyond repair if I stayed in New York and continued to live in the role of my old identity as a rejected woman without hope.

I would stop along the highway for periods of rest and meditation, wishing I could find a formula along the way to remove this root of bitterness and hurt. I could only find seeds of doubt planted by the enemy. I could not help doubting the security and validity of my journey...*No.* I cannot look back; those doors behind me are closed tight and my loved ones all have hearts of stone. *No.* There is no turning back.

Fear of the future can immobilize you and keep you from making the plans that help you rebuild your life. I knew it would take a miracle to rebuild my shattered life, but where could I find a miracle on a lonely highway, all alone, with no one to talk to but God? I was like a city shattered by an earthquake and needing to be rebuilt piece by piece.

After my first long day's drive on America's major highway I-95 heading south from Maryland, I was looking for a Days Inn motel to retire for the night. After seven hours of lonely driving, I pulled off at the first Days Inn, parked my car in the parking lot and went into the dining room first to have a meal. I sat next to a couple who couldn't help but notice me, alone, tired and depressed-looking. It was as if God planted them there to show me love and to make me feel someone recognized my hurt and felt my pain.

They introduced themselves as Mr. and Mrs. Walsh, an Irish American couple from Boston. They shared with me that they were on their way to a Christian Retreat Center in North Carolina for a week and invited me to come along with them. "Well," I thought, "if they are driving all that way to spend a week at a Christian retreat, there must be something there that I am not aware of." I decided to try it out.

It was so unusual to find people with such love and concern after weathering such storms of hate and rejection. They were concerned about my driving alone on the highway under such emotional stress and without the Lord in my life...

A New Day Has Dawned; the Day of My Salvation: Sept. 26, 1978

When we got to the Christian Village that night, we attended the service that was already in progress. It was the Irish-born evangelist "Bob Gass" who conducted the service. When I walked in and heard that Irish accent, I felt right at home. I could relate to him. I knew that God led me there for a reason. It seemed He always knew where I was, but I did not know where He was.

That service was so different, the presence of God was so real, I felt the anointing even though I did not understand where it came from or what it meant.

Bob asked for a testimony. I wanted to ask: What is that? Being raised in the Catholic Church, we were programmed not to talk in church, never mind asking or answering questions. I was not sure what a testimony was or what significance it served to the service. Then he asked if anyone had anything good happen to him or her today. Oh yes, my hand went up for that and I shared how the Lord put this couple in my path that led me to the house of the Lord tonight. I aroused great applause, but I did not have the courage to share the hurt and trauma within me.

I looked around and all I could feel was love from this body of people, which was a great balm to heal my wounds. No one, only God, knew what I was going through that night. I kept wondering if I would ever recover and start over. Only a miracle from God could set me free and put me on my feet again.

I had experienced one of the hardest and most emotional crises any human being can face. I know the heartache of that time. I know what it is to be devastated, wounded and alone on the highway of life.

Psalm 119:71

It is good for me that I have been afflicted; that I might learn Thy statutes.

To fail just about as miserably as any woman can fail: I have been there. If I hadn't found the Lord and invited Him into my life that night, my life would have crumbled. Little did I know that God was going to turn it around. I had the determination and the faith that God would help me weather the hurt, pain and frustration. But little did I know that God had a plan to use my suffering, to create within me the person He intended me to be and to turn my crisis into a "Joseph" experience. God does not allow us to go through anything He cannot use to glorify His name.

One of the things I learned from Bob Gass' message that night, was when he said, "If you have no direction in your life, if you don't know where you are going, any road will take you there." That was me. I sure could relate to that. He also stated that life does not begin at 40, it begins when you meet *Jesus*. That also ministered to me. I knew in my wounded heart that was why I was there, to meet Jesus, but how? As Bob led into the invitation for salvation, he said, "If you don't know *Jesus*, don't leave here tonight without Him." I thought I had known Him all my life, but I hadn't known Him personally. I could not relate to the scriptures Bob quoted, as I had never read the Bible. I was spiritually ignorant. I had never heard of the salvation plan; I thought salvation was automatic for the church. Bob planted the seed of salvation in my life that night and aroused my curiosity in the spirit.

After the service that night, we went out to have a midnight snack. I had such a peace, like something had lifted off of me, I knew it was something I never had felt before. I knew the service was different from anything I had ever attended before.

When I returned to the hotel, the Lord put a nice Christian lady in my path, Ruth May from Rockville, Maryland, who shared the four spiritual laws with me. She shared scriptures with me, as well as her testimony and her experience in the baptism of the Holy Spirit. We fellowshipped well into the early hours. When she shared John 3:3 with me, I knew in my heart that's what I had been searching for all my life: security and assurance of the Kingdom of Heaven.

However, my mind could consume only so much that night. I knew I had found a treasure, but I only accepted salvation so I would be sure of going to Heaven. I knew then that this world was not my home. So through my suffering I had found my way to eternity.

Little did I know then the plans the Lord had for me down the road.

As I shared my crisis with Ruth, she showed such love and compassion for me, driving alone on American highways in distress. So she introduced me to a couple from Florida that she met at the retreat, Mildred and Claude Branch, who also showed love and compassion for me. They invited me to drive behind them on the way to Tampa, which was my destination. We stayed at the same motel that night, ate dinner together and fellowshipped. They shared their address and telephone number with me and invited me to visit them.

A few days after my arrival in Tampa, I went to visit them in their mobile home in Thonotosasso, Florida. Mildred ministered to me all evening, and Claude played tapes. After I shared my crisis with them, they both read me some scriptures.

Lamentations 3:26

It is good that a man should both hope and quietly wait for the salvation of the Lord.

The one thing Mildred shared that I never forgot was that, when we invite the Lord into our lives and allow Him to run it for us, we will experience a whole new life. He will turn all our suffering around and use us to help others. He will equip us with His gifts so we will have the tools to evangelize a hurting world. Even though I did not understand what she was saying, it stayed with me until I reaped the fruits of those words.

Ruth May became a lifetime friend. I visited with her and her late husband Gordan many times in Maryland. Ruth has watched the power of God move in my life over the years. The seed she planted in my life grew and blossomed after I learned to walk in God's will and to fill my life with significant accomplishments. My crisis became a learning process as I grew through the pain. I grew in wisdom and knowledge that I never could otherwise have found.

There is a segment of scripture that Paul wrote in Philippians 4:4-19 about learning to accept where you are. "Not that I speak in respect of want: for I have learned, in whatsoever state I am, therewith to be content" (v. 11). Paul had experienced numerous shipwrecks, anger, mobs, trials and imprisonments. He was seldom out of a crisis. Somehow God gave him a spirit of confidence to let him know that wherever he was at any given moment in his life was all right; not always comfortable, but right.

We have all heard the slogan, "bloom where you are planted." I had to apply it in my life in my present situation. Paul showed a good example of his strength by doing some of his blooming while he was imprisoned. He longed to be free, but he used his experience to win some of his captors to a faith in Christ. He applied the secret in verse 13, "I can do all things through Christ which strengtheneth me." Paul was not growing on his own. Neither was I. God was infusing him daily with the strength he needed.

God blessed me with that same growth-producing strength, for no one else could do my growing for me. In verse 19 Paul talks about building. He says, "But my God shall supply all your need according to his riches in glory by Christ Jesus." You cannot build anything until God supplies you with the materials. His building design for our lives is in the area of supplying the things we need, rather than the things we want.

Many newly divorced people cannot move ahead with their lives because they don't have everything, personally and materially, they had before divorce interrupted their journey. The problem is, they can see what they don't have rather than what God does have. Scripture tells us, "But seek first His kingdom and His righteousness, and all these things will be given to you as well" (Matt. 6:33 NIV). Those are the promises regarding God's supplying our construction materials. Accepting who we are and growing and building are an important part of the process of creating a new identity. They help set us free from the growing threat of loneliness.

Chapter 5

My First Christmas Alone with Jesus

I Peter 4:12-13

Beloved, think it not strange concerning the fiery trial which is to try you, as though some strange thing happened unto you: but rejoice, inasmuch as ye are partakers of Christ's sufferings; that, when His glory shall be revealed, ye may be glad also with exceeding joy.

In December '78, I was working as a waitress at the Breakers Hotel in Palm Beach, which was very elite and had a delightful tourist atmosphere. But my first Christmas without a family or a home of my own took me through another journey of pain and heartache, which never seemed to end. After 21 years of marriage and raising three children, suffering four miscarriages and six major surgeries and losing my life-long possessions, I now found myself spending my first Christmas Eve alone with Jesus. I sure was under a fiery trial and I had no choice but to believe that I was a partaker in Christ's suffering.

With every circumstance comes the provision for total victory. I went to work that Christmas Eve from 5 p.m. till midnight. Most of the waitresses were in a festive mood, discussing the different Christmas parties they were going to after work. Some of them came in with gift-wrapped packages, party dresses and fancy hairdos, ready for a festive evening of fun and celebration. Not one of them invited me to come along or asked me if I had family to join me in celebrating Christmas.

Rejection and loneliness tried to creep in again. But when midnight approached and the dining room emptied out, I checked out, got into my car and drove down Ocean Avenue to St. Edward's Church. I got into midnight mass at 12:10, just as the choir was singing songs of love and truth— praises to the King of kings. The church was full of God's people all in a festive spirit. The altar was decorated so colorfully with poinsettia. The presence of God was so real. I felt a healing process taking place within my lonely heart. As I joined in the singing of the Christmas carols, I felt a breaking in my wounded spirit. How could I feel so rejected a couple of hours earlier when I was not invited to a worldly party? The Lord had a plan for me that night and I almost missed it.

When the priest gave the message from the Book of Luke, relating to Mary being in labor with our Savior that night long ago, walking from door to door looking for a place to lay her head to give birth to the baby Jesus, my attitude started to change. Our heavenly Father could have provided a nice place for Mary that night, like the one He provided for me in my hour of distress, the night of my eviction. But His purpose was to program our selfish carnal minds to trust in Him and Him only.

The Lord showed me that night that my struggle through my first lonely Christmas could not compare with Mary's hardship that night to give birth to the child that made Christmas possible and so special to all generations.

The miracle of Christmas took on new meaning in my life. I no longer looked upon it as a time for glittering lights on the tree and doorways, stockings hanging by the chimney, festive parties, family gatherings and Santa Claus idolatry.

The memory of my first Christmas alone on the ocean of Palm Beach cannot be erased even with time, laughter or tears. It led me to a new aware-ness in Christ Jesus, whose birthday we celebrate on that beautiful night. It also made me aware of the reason the stockings I hung for Santa Claus as a child were always empty, while the children of the rest of my community enjoyed the fruits of that Yuletide tradition.

James 1:17 (NIV)

Every good and perfect gift is from above, coming down from the Father of the heavenly lights, who does not change like shifting shadows.

I never exchange Christmas gifts anymore. I just send gifts to those whom I don't expect to reciprocate, as I realize it is more blessed to give than to receive. When we plant seed into each other's lives, we reap a harvest far beyond our gifts.

The true miracle of Christmas is *hope, faith* and *love*. These are the gifts the Christ Child brought to all of us from Heaven above.

A New Year Has Dawned in January '79

Christmas Eve taught me one of the greatest lessons any of us could ever experience. Even though I still had not found a way to fill the empti-ness in my life, I was beginning to feel total de-pendence on God.

Sometimes I wanted to scream out, "Where are You hiding, Lord? Don't You care about my pain? How could You permit such a thing to happen to me?"

How could He be "God" and not have the power to prevent such a disaster? What was it I needed to do, to see God's purpose for all of this?

By this time I had realized that self-pity was one of the worst stumbling blocks to the healing and restoration of my crisis. I was also beginning to understand what *deadly poison* the "poor me" attitude was, but what do you do with the pain of rejection and abandonment?

Moving to Florida was like moving to a new land away from home. It was like when I emigrated from Ireland to America as a teenager, to make a new life, new friends and new roots in new territory, to go through intense growth periods of my new life.

It was now four months since I had left New York. I longed to see my children again, but had no idea when I would get up the courage to make the trip.

On January 20th, my 15-year-old nephew Denis Cameron was killed by a car in the streets of Brooklyn, New York. As the tragic news reached me, the Lord gave me the courage to fly up for the memorial services, which entailed a large family gathering. This gave me a chance to be united with my three children again.

2 Corinthians 4:8-9 (NIV)

We are hard pressed on every side, but not crushed; perplexed, but not in despair; persecuted, but not abandoned; struck down, but not destroyed.

I spent a few days with my sister, Bridie, and her family to help soothe their wounds in their time of grief. Now I saw suffering in a whole new light. I compared Bridie's grief with my crisis. They were both a loss and both caused tears, pain and heartache. A child's life and a marriage were shattered to pieces by the work of the enemy.

Death is eternal, and so is the pain of divorce. Grief and loss are unavoidable, yet the way we grieve and the length of time we suffer is truly our choice. As Paul says in that scripture, we are hard pressed but not crushed, perplexed but not in despair, persecuted but not abandoned, struck down but not destroyed.

I've heard it said so many times that, when we need more light on our path, God will provide. So we are no longer in charge. We must let go of the past to give God enough room to work in our crises. No matter what the circumstances are, God is bigger than any crisis we have. He can move any mountain. Through Him we can heal, recover and go on living and make that period a time of becoming. Seeing ourselves as victims weakens us and paralyzes our emotions.

My sister had so many people left with whom to share her grief: her husband, her daughter, her son and a large circle of friends. She also had a beautiful home. She was not alone on the highway of life, homeless and rejected.

I returned to Florida to face another lonely spell, feeling desperate about my life, which seemed to be going nowhere. But I found a great spiritual bonanza there. My anger about pain was beginning to melt as I came to know Jesus more intimately. His grace was a means of becoming, and even though I was still homeless and abandoned, I was feeling His comfort and joy.

I could now relate to Mary's sufferings and trials. I realized that her son Jesus who died on the cross for my suffering, my healing and my salvation, also went through a time of extreme rejection. But it did not destroy Him. He knew the purpose of His suffering. Now I am beginning to feel that my suffering also has a purpose.

Jesus Cares about Our Suffering

The image Jesus left with the world, "the Cross," is proof that He cares about our pain. That lonely bleeding figure which hung on that cross expressed enough *love* for all the pain and suffering of the world.

John 3:16 (NIV)

For God so loved the world that He gave His one and only Son, that whoever believes in Him shall not perish but have eternal life.

Many divorced, hurting women are so defeated. They have spent years bobbing through life like corks on the water, hoping someone will walk into their lives and take over their hurts.

The cross became real to me in my suffering. That healing blood that was shed at Calvary for all mankind is the only prescription I found on my journey to recovery.

Chapter 6

My Family Unit

Acts 2:38-39

> *Then Peter said unto them, Repent, and be baptized every one of you in the name of Jesus Christ for the remission of sins, and ye shall receive the gift of the Holy Ghost. For the promise is unto you, and to **your children**, and to all that are afar off, even as many as the Lord our God shall call.*

My Son Anthony's Graduation

In June '79, I made my next trip to New York for Anthony's high school graduation, another occasion to be united with family.

I finished my waitressing job in Palm Beach for the season and secured a waitressing job in the

Washington Hotel, which was located in the White Mountains of New Hampshire. I secured a job for Anthony also, so he could spend the summer with me. He was still struggling through his teens, had just gotten his driver's license and was seeking a working career while attending college.

Later that summer I made a trip to Ireland with the Mayo Association of New York, which was celebrating its centennial anniversary. I took my Aunt Betty (Regan) Burbidge of New Jersey with me. It was her first trip to her homeland in 53 years. There she was united with her sister Monica and two brothers, John and Dan. It was a painful trip for me, visiting relatives and old friends and trying to pose as a single person again, trying to pretend I was healed of the pain when the wounds were still festering.

What do we do with the pain? I refused to have pity parties. God is bigger than any problem we have. Jesus says He lives so I can have tomorrow.

I had to overcome the dislike of my new title as well. I did not like to be referred to as a "divorced woman." I would ask myself, "Who am I? Where do I go from here? Is life so empty? Do I just fill space? I know God did not create me just to go on suffering; He must have a purpose in all this...." After a long struggle with this, I read Catherine Marshall's book, *How to Live Again.* I gained some strength from that book; it gave me new insight. I learned to be just myself and wait on the Lord.

I knew God accepted me just where I was at. If He hadn't, He would not have picked me up on that lonely highway and filled me with His love, His power and His strength. He became my whole source of supply. So if the God of the universe loves me, who cares what the rest of the world thinks of me.

That was a wonderful revelation and a tremendous help in getting me through the transition from grief to relief and out into the sunshine again.

When I got back to New York after that Ireland trip, the stale taste of family rejection and of rebellious spirits haunted me again. I knew I had to get out from under it. God was dealing with me in this area and I knew I had to let go of the past, but it didn't happen overnight. I knew that in God's time the sharp edge would wear off. Meanwhile He gave me the strength to weather the storm and eventually separate myself from the torture of the past.

I returned to Florida for another winter. I had made friends there from the previous season. I got deeply involved in the Charismatic prayer groups and church activities, which fulfilled my spiritual needs as I began to grow in the love and admonition of the Lord. Every day was a new venture in Him. He became the eminent part of my life.

Restaurant business dies in Florida in the summer season, so waitresses have to seek employment in the resorts up north. Again I secured a job in Cape Cod for the season of 1980.

God Has Multiplied My Family to Ten Children

My two daughters, Lillian and Kathy, are now in their 30's. They are busy mothers to my five grandsons. Lillian's husband, Brian Murphy, is a native of New Ross, County Wexford, Ireland. He is one of eight children. He and Lillian have three boys: Sean, aged 11; Kieran, aged 9; and Brendan, aged 5.

Kathy's husband, Pat O'Brien, is also a native of New Ross, County Wexford. He comes from a family of seven brothers and one sister. He and Kathy have two boys: Johnny, who is now three and a half and baby Evan, who was born during the editing of this book.

These add up to five grandsons and two sons-in-law, and my son Anthony and my two daughters make it ten children. It is such a blessing to see the extension of your life's blood multiplied in numbers.

Both families reside in Bronx, New York. All nine of them came to Florida to visit Disneyworld and to celebrate my 60th birthday. God blessed our time together. It was a beautiful time of sharing. I praise God for such a loving relationship. God can still mend the broken pieces in family relationshps.

My two sisters, Helena and Bridie, also live in New York. Helena and her husband, John McDermott, raised five children, four boys and one girl. Their daughter, Madeline, just got married to a young Irish man, Des Dillion.

Bridie's husband went home to be with the Lord three years ago. Her son, daughter and granddaughter reside with her in Brooklyn, New York. Bridie spent a month here in Florida with me this summer, in 1992.

Praise God for family relationships.

Chapter 7

Another Blow: Without Medical Insurance

Matthew 5:44-45

But I say unto you, Love your enemies, bless them that curse you, do good to them that hate you, and pray for them which despitefully use you, and persecute you; that ye may be the children of your Father which is in heaven: for He maketh His sun to rise on the evil and on the good, and sendeth rain on the just and on the unjust.

While I was in a hospital bed, I found out that I had no medical insurance. It was another blow, but God provided all my needs.

It was while I was in New York, the summer of 1980, that I was hospitalized with a kidney stone. After lying in bed for four days, going through the routine tests, I was ready for discharge when the worst news of all hit me. The admitting office informed me that my hospitalization coverage had been terminated by my ex-husband. Fear gripped me like never before. I could hardly hear the words that the man spoke to me. The spirit of rejection had another bat at me. I was hit with another blow.

The carpet was pulled right out from under me now. It was one thing to be thrown out on the street like a bag of broken pottery after being stripped of everything I had ever possessed. Now I was lying on a hospital bed without medical coverage.

If Tony had only notified me, I could have picked up the policy at a very small monthly payment. He had an excellent plan with the Bus Co. for major medical, etc., but God had a better plan for me. However, first I had to be obedient to Matthew 5:44-45. Forgive! Love your enemies. Vengeance is Mine, saith the Lord. I will repay! (Rom. 12:19).

A great freedom welled up inside of me as soon as I forgave him. Moments later the phone rang. It was the man in the office again, alerting me to the possibility that I could qualify for Medicaid. I thought that was for the poor, the downtrodden and the homeless. Seemingly that's where I was at: no home, no husband, no job, no alimony and no medical coverage. Talk about being stripped to the bone. I've been there. But again the Lord came to my rescue. I filled out the application and I qualified for the benefit.

We serve an awesome God. No one else could meet my needs and carry me through the storms that He brought me through. I knew for sure then that His hand was upon me. He met me on the Damascus road. I knew that somewhere down the road I was headed for a better life. I already felt the recovery as He led me out of the wilderness and darkness and into His marvelous light. What looked impossible became possible; He became my husband and my provider.

Matthew 3:10 tells us that the axe is laid at the root. If there is a root of rejection still operating in your life, release it. Forgive your enemies and allow God to move that which would produce bad fruit.

It is not what we are and it is not what we possess. It is what God can make of us. He becomes strong in our weakness. When God looks down upon man, He does not look at him for what he is, but for what He can transform his life into.

I had no idea during this fearful storm why He was so merciful to me. Now I realize He was depending on what He could make of me. I was willing to surrender my total being completely into His hands, all that I was and just as I was. He knew that someday I would go forth and glorify His name and write my story for the healing of other rejected women who have not yet come to know Him.

Luke 4:18 tells us that Jesus came to set at liberty those that are bruised. How could He do that? It is because Jesus Himself was bruised and rejected. He was despised and rejected by His own people, just as I was rejected by my family. But because He bore my grief and sorrow and rejection at Calvary, healing was available to me. His love was sufficient to heal my rejection and set me free.

When Jesus came into my life, I became an overcomer. Yet I had to decrease so He could increase in me and use me for the healing of other rejected women.

Satan has commissioned his demonic forces to bruise us in every way possible. Divorce, broken homes, drugs, sexual assault, peer pressure and our very own society are tools he uses to bruise the people of God. God is calling us today to root out, pull down, destroy and tear down every root which produces bad fruit in our lives so that He can build and plant.

Chapter 8

My Journey Across America

I drove coast to coast through the lower 48 states and spent a season in Alaska and Hawaii; a seven-year adventure with Jesus as my pilot.

In the fall of 1980, I started out from New York to drive coast to coast. I knew now that I had the gift of driving and the Holy Spirit inspired me on this venture. I made the Lord the pilot of my car, since it was easier for me to be the co-pilot. I had a Mercury Monarch with high mileage, but I had no fear since my pilot was in control of my safety and of all my needs.

I have relatives and friends all over America, whom I visited on my way. I had no idea where my destination was or what lay ahead. I didn't even know I would travel all 50 states, but the Lord kept opening doors for me.

I had to work my way through the country, so I lived and worked in every major city. Finding employment was never a problem. Sometimes I'd go into a city where I had no contacts, but as soon as I went to the house of the Lord I had an instant family.

When you belong to the family of God, His people are everywhere and He allows your paths to cross, for He knows when two or more of His people are joined together in His name, He is there in their midst and His sheep hear His voice. (See Matthew 18:20 and John 10:4.)

I saw America and all its beauty, which is God's creation. I visited every state capital, every monument of interest, every national park, including the Rocky Mountain National Park, the Petrified Forest, the Grand Canyon, Death Valley, Yellowstone National Park, Lake Tahoe...you name it. It was a very educational trip, a trip few Americans have experienced.

I met the most interesting people, from all walks of life, who opened their hearts and shared their homes and their love with me. Most of them were blessed by my testimony and so excited about my venture, they would call their friends in the next city to secure contacts for me on my journey. I was beginning to see the hand of God working out my provision.

Do You Drive Alone?

The question that was most often asked of me was, "Do you drive alone?" "Oh no! I never drive alone, I always have my pilot with me," I'd answer.

They would look into my car to see who the pilot was. "Oh no! *Jesus* is my pilot all the time, all across America, over the mountains and through the desert. There is no way I could make it alone across this land."

"But how do you entertain yourself for those long hours behind the wheel?"

I would talk to Him, sing and praise Him, listen to Christian tapes and, when I discovered it, Christian radio.

The first major city I spent time in was Denver, Colorado. I had driven 1,960 miles from New York after visiting relatives in Michigan and friends in Des Moines, Iowa, on my way.

My cousin Peggie Shea and her husband and children lived in Lakewood, north of Denver. I secured employment there at Stouffer's Inn for six weeks. I toured all that beautiful area while I was there. I truly enjoyed the foliage season blooming so colorfully on the mountains. The purple heather reminded me of the bogs of Ireland. Time passed very quickly for me there between visiting my lovely cousins, sight-seeing and working.

After six weeks I continued my journey through Colorado Springs, then south to Walsenberg and west to Cortz, via Mesa Verde National Park, and continued south through the Indian Reservation to the only point in the U.S. where four states meet. This spot is called the four-state corner, where Arizona, New Mexico, Colorado and Utah adjoin.

I had left colorful Colorado far behind and was now into the desert and Indian country. I had no contacts in this area, but I never entertained fear. I was never afraid of being alone because *alone* is a time of becoming.

Strangers in strange lands are lonely; that's part of the price. But you can be lonely in a marriage. You can be lonely in a crowd. Loneliness can be a wilderness experience. Through the pain of loneliness God can get our attention. I choose my lonely times to be a pathway to God.

In no time I was in Arizona, the valley of the sun, visiting the Grand Canyon National Park. This was the most exciting spot of the trip so far.

Two days later I reached Phoenix where I visited Tom and Peggie Mullins, whom I met accidently by calling the wrong number. Through them I got a house-sitting job for six weeks and also secured a waitressing job at the Carefree Inn, a beautiful resort. The Lord continued to supply all my needs by going before me and opening all the doors.

I met some lovely people in this area through the Mullins family. I also visited Scotsdale, Sun City, Mesa, Glendale, Tempe and the famous "Wigwam" Country Club resort in "Litchfield Park." I also attended the Catholic Charismatic prayer groups there.

I found Jesus people in every city.

My next city was Las Vegas, a short three-hour drive through the desert. It was so hot, the windshield wipers of my car melted. I looked around at the other motorists to see if theirs had melted, and I noticed none of the cars had wipers. I asked the attendant at the gas station why that was so and he said, "We don't need any in the desert because it never rains."

I stayed a week in Las Vegas with Ruth Watkins, a lovely Christian lady I met through her sister-in-law in Phoenix. I had run out of relatives in this area, but God was still opening doors for me.

Ruth drove me through the strip that first night to see the lights. What a fairyland; all the glitter and glamour I had seen in the movies for years became a reality. I visited all the casinos, took in a few shows and toured Hoover Dam. I would have loved to stay longer and get a waitressing job, but they were all sewed up with the unions. I knew I could never be a poker dealer or a dice thrower. My Christian principles would not allow me to gamble.

Billy Graham's crusade was coming to town that week also. The city was plastered with posters and thousands were pouring in for the service. I realized that Jesus people are everywhere, even in Las Vegas.

The Watkins became lifetime friends. I visited them again five years later when my brother John Carney moved there.

California, Here I Come

The next 18 months I spent in southern California. I also found it hard to secure waitressing work there because of the unions. I was over 50, and most fancy restaurants preferred the mini-skirt waitress. I searched the job market in the newspaper and found a domestic agency. This agency provided me with a live-in companion position, which not only provided me with a good salary, but also nice living quarters. So I was able to tour all of the Hollywood and Beverly Hills section, as well as visit relatives and Irish friends in

L.A., San Diego, Santa Monica and Malibu, which were beautiful historic areas. I spent some memorable visits with Ann Gregg and her husband and children; with John Hanley and his wife and children; with Kathleen Glynn and Tom and their two sons; and with Una and Vincent Hanley.

I moved to San Francisco in '82: the city of St. Francis with all its hills and bays and bridges, its trolley cars, red woods and Fishermen's Wharf. I loved it. I found myself a nice companion job with a sweet lady in Piedmont, which was over the Bay Bridge and up on the side of a mountain where I could view all of San Francisco and the Bay.

While I lived there, I spent a lot of time with Joe and Ellen Glynn and their daughters. Joe is from my hometown. His wife and family became life-long friends. Also, Joe's Aunt Winnie Garrity, who is now 93, became a special friend. I met a large circle of new Irish friends and attended many Irish functions there with the Glynns. It was a very special time of fellowship.

While I was there I also spent a season in Hawaii on a companion job for five months. Before I returned, I took a month's vacation to Australia and New Zealand.

I spent the summer of '83 in Anchorage, Alaska. I drove from San Francisco to Seattle, Washington, left my car with Irish friends there and flew to

Anchorage. The Lord went before me again and opened a great door so I could work for three months. During that time I visited Fairbanks, took a cruise of the glaciers and took a trip to Mt. McKinley National Park. Alaska was a neat experience.

When I got back to Seattle, I went to Vancouver, British Columbia, visiting people I had met in Hawaii. In the fall of '83, I started my return trip back east, through Montana, Wyoming, Utah, North Dakota, South Dakota, Minnesota, Wisconsin and Illinois, visiting people and places all the way. When I reached Chicago, I visited Rita Connolly, an old friend from my school days.

Rita and her husband Ray have 13 children: 10 girls and 3 boys. Their daughter Mary got married while I was there. What a special wedding that was, with ten sisters in the bridal party. I spent a lot of quality time in their home. They are a God-chosen family.

I also had great fellowship with Peggie and Dom Sharkey. I spent several weekends at their home. I also spent time with Eileen and Jim Staunton. We shared a great spiritual and social life together.

I secured employment in Chicago as a nanny to the governor's daughter for a season. It was nice to explore the Governor's Mansion, be chauffeured by a state trooper and enjoy some special privileges.

I spent the summer of '84 in Bar Harbour, Maine, where I secured a waitressing job with Testa's, whom I had also worked for in Palm Beach. I explored the quaintness of the lifestyle in Maine. The mountains, Acadia National Park and Desert Island were so scenic. I spent much time enjoying the beauty of it all. I also found a great spiritual life there, and great prayer partners. When my job finished in October, the foliage season was in full bloom in the mountains and all along the countryside.

My next move was to Texas, but I had to cover all the southern states on my way. So I decided to take the long route through Canada. From Maine I drove north to Quebec, on to Montreal and into Toronto where I visited the Sweeneys and the Byrnes from my hometown in Ireland. I took a few days to tour the city before starting out for the States again. I entered the U.S. through Windsor bridge into Detroit, where I visited more Irish friends.

Now, for the long road south, my goal was to reach the World's Fair in New Orleans. I visited people all the way through Indiana, Kentucky, Tennessee, Alabama, Mississippi and into Louisiana. I stayed with a lady I met in Maine for five days while I visited the World's Fair. It was now close to 3,000 miles since I left Maine. It was time to get off the road and settle into a job again for another few months.

I drove into Texas, where I spent two weeks in Houston, three months in San Antonio and four months in Dallas. Jesus people were everywhere in Texas. I had a great spiritual life there.

My Odyssey Came to an End in Magnolia, Arkansas

While I was in Dallas, I finally visited my 50th state: Arkansas. An Arkansas lady I met in Hawaii, Ruby Dillard, was intrigued with my venture. She told me that if I ever made it to her hometown, I could be her houseguest. The day came when I rang her from Dallas and told her I had only one state left to finish my odyssey. She was so excited, she contacted the mayor of that city and told him about this adventurous lady she had met. He showed a desire to interview me and have me share my story with the press. As a result, I made the front page of their local newspaper the next morning. Thus my story was birthed and my tour of the 50 states was far behind, to become a lifetime memory of this beautiful land.

I really had planned to write a book on my venture at that time, but got sidetracked with all the wonderful things that happened to my life since then. In fact, I was invited to be on a TV show called "Incredible People." It was about people who did rare things. However, before I got called, the show went off the air. They could not find enough contestants who did crazy things.

Now, seven years later, I still have great memories of not just the beautiful America that I experienced firsthand, but also of the beautiful people who encouraged me with their love and sheltered me on my journey. They have a special significance in my personal odyssey. Most of all, I came to realize what total dependence on the Lord was like. That was so meaningful to me in the dry periods. I also came to a new awareness of myself and learned to survive any crisis through the power of my God. I know for sure that He has a plan for my life and that He will guide me every step of the way as I walk it out.

Irish-born woman tours states

Mary Cunnane began an adventure in 1978 when she left her home state of New York and took to America's highways.

The Ireland native said she has since traveled from coast to coast in her quest to visit all 50 states and all the nation's major cities. Arkansas was her 50th state to visit. This week Cunnane was the guest of Ruby Dillard of Magnolia.

Cunnane said she logged 95,200 on one car and 22,000 on another during her seven-year odyssey. The traveler said she now plans to write a book about her adventures on America's highways.

Magnolian Ruby Dillard (from left) looks on as her guest, Ireland native Mary Cunnane of New York, is greeted by Magnolia Mayor George Wheatley. Visiting Arkansas marked the completion of a goal Cunnane had set of seeing all 50 states.

Chapter 9

How I Found the Holy Spirit

While I was in southern California, I discovered TBN, 24-hour Christian TV. I watched it day and night, every chance I got. That is where I got the foundation for my biblical walk.

I was so spiritually ignorant. I had never read the Bible; I did not know that laypeople could receive spiritual gifts to minister to the Body of Christ. I thought you had to be a priest to do that. I heard a lot about the anointing and praying in tongues, but I did not think all that was for Catholic people. I rejected it for years since I never heard anyone in the Catholic Church use any of these gifts. I had such a fear of getting involved in anything that was not of my church.

When I was in Chicago, Peggie and Dom Sharkey took me to a healing service in a Catholic Church given by a laywoman, "Barbara O'Malley." This was new to me. We Catholics were brought up to believe that God did not use women in the church.

The Lord dealt with my beliefs that night. As soon as I got into the service, I felt the anointing. I didn't know what it was, but I knew it was something I had never felt before. I heard people praying in tongues, singing in tongues and falling in the Spirit. I could not believe I was in a Catholic Church.

As soon as Barbara laid hands on me, I was slain in the Spirit for the first time. While I was resting in the Spirit, I began to pray in tongues. God really showed me that the gift of the Holy Spirit was for everyone, regardless of his or her denomination.

I was on fire for days, praying in my new prayer language, playing tapes I had received on the subject and reading all the books I could get hold of about the power of the Holy Spirit and the changes it makes in a person's life.

The hardest part was when I would share it with Catholic friends and Irish friends. They would say, "What is that? That is not Catholic. What are you into?" They tried to discourage me by telling me it was a new religion, but I kept saying, "I found it in the Catholic Church, so it must be all right."

There was only one thing left for me to do now, before the enemy could try to rob me of this gift. That was to get into the Word and study. I knew that was where I would find the truth, and the truth would set me free. (See John 8:32.)

When I read these scriptures...

Proverbs 20:27

The spirit of man is the candle of the Lord, searching all the inward parts of the belly.

Proverbs 1:22-23

How long, ye simple ones, will ye love simplicity? and the scorners delight in their scorning, and fools hate knowledge? Turn you at my reproof: behold, I will pour out my spirit unto you, I will make known my words unto you.

I got the message and I became aware that the Holy Spirit was for me. So the glory continued. The presence of the Lord did not depart; it actually intensified. The Word became more real. My prayer life became more powerful. I also became aware that the Holy Spirit does not dwell in a building or in an edifice, but only in the spirit of man. That's the only way He can operate on this earth. We are His hands, His feet and His mouthpiece. Our bodies are the temple of the Holy Spirit. That really excited me.

Even though the Spirit of God was now dwelling in my temple, I did not know there were seven gifts and nine fruits of the Holy Spirit. Still, God started to pour gift after gift upon me before I understood how to use them. Those of you who have received the gift of tongues know that it does not come with instructions. I had no idea what the purpose of it was or how to use it.

Three weeks after I received the gift of tongues, I was invited to Baby Martin Murphy's christening. The baby's Dad was from my homeland of Bekan, Ireland. As I looked in the bassinet at the baby, I noticed that one of his eyes was very red and teary. I asked the grandmother, who was next to me, what it was. She said that he was born with a weeping tear duct and that the doctors couldn't do anything about it until he was old enough for surgery. A little voice inside of me spoke and said, "Lay hands on him; pray for his healing." I looked around to see how many people were watching and I thought, "No way; I am not in this business. I am not Barbara O'Malley."

At this point I did not know that Jesus did the healing through the work of the Holy Spirit within me. I was only the vessel He uses to lay hands on the sick. It is the Spirit that completes the process of healing. But since I did not fully understand, I asked the mother of the baby, Eileen Murphy, to take him into the kitchen so I could pray for him in private. Two days later Eileen called me, all excited that Baby Martin's eye was completely healed. Little did I realize then that my healing ministry had just taken root.

I called Barbara O'Malley the next day to tell her what happened. She said, "Praise God, Mary, you have the gift of healing." I cried with excitement. But I could not comprehend what was happening to me. I really thought God had made a mistake and given this gift to the wrong person. Why should He choose me? I was a nobody all my life—a rejected orphan, a rejected wife and a rejected mother. I couldn't help myself, and now He chose me to use His healing power.

In the months ahead He worked quite a few miracles through me. One time I went to a hospital to pray for a lady who had emphysema. She was already on life support. I laid hands on her in Jesus' name and she was miraculously healed. I knew then that God had touched my life and I did not question why.

All those years I suffered through the spirit of rejection, He was nurturing me and preparing me for such a time as this. James 2:26 tells us, "For the body without the spirit is dead, so faith without works is dead also." I knew I had to nourish my faith in His Word, for He promised that signs and wonders would follow those who have faith in His Word. (See Mark 16:17.)

When my old friends opposed my new-found life, I could relate to their feelings, for the carnal mind cannot comprehend the things of the spirit because it is foolishness to them. But God cannot be mocked; a man reaps what he sows. Yet, those who are led by the Spirit are no longer under condemnation.

When my brother John came to visit me last year, he asked me if I realized that I had lost all my old friends and relatives because of this silly Charismatic thing I was into. I told him, "I did not apply for these gifts. God chose to bless me with them and I have to make a decision to either serve God or serve man."

The Lord reminded me that I have not lost any of those people; rather they have lost me. They are looking for the *old* Mary, the rejected woman. They don't recognize the new-found life that God redeemed, restored and made whole.

Romans 8:18 reminds us that the sufferings of this present time are not worthy to be compared with the glory which will be revealed in us.

We have the power to choose our own destiny; the power of life or death, victory or defeat.

Chapter 10

My Loveless Life as a Child

Now that you have read about my life after divorce, I am sure you would like to know what my childhood was like. Needless to say, it was a love-less life of rejection. My mother died when I was 17 months old and my brother only 10 weeks old. She was breast-feeding him when she was struck down with typhoid fever.

My Dad suffered a painful cross. Because the fever was so contagious, no one would come into his farmhouse to help him with his two babies. I do believe the spirit of rejection attached itself to me during this time, even at such an early age.

Thank God for Dad's two sisters who came to his rescue. My Aunt Annie O'Dea cared for me and my Aunt Mary Jordan cared for John.

My Dad remarried when I was about three years old. I remember the day I was taken away from my aunt and uncle, the parents I had come to know and love. My Dad came to take me home to my new Mom. He never explained where I was going or why; he just picked me up like a package and brought me to the old home. He never introduced me to my new Mom or explained to me who she was or why I was taken to her. And she herself could have taken me in her arms, given me a hug and told me she loved me. She didn't. That relationship never changed for the rest of my childhood.

The transition from one home to another is still vivid in my memory. I may have been only a little child, but my mind was mature enough to know that my life was interrupted without an explanation. I saw my new Mom as a stranger, without any affection. I was like a lost child in a world without love. As I grew older, the spirit of rejection became more evident to me. It was not because of my step-mother; the root of rejection had been planted in my life before she entered it. She was not the root cause.

The past always affects the future. Children must hear loving words of acceptance to develop properly. The effects of emotional abuse or abandonment can be devastating and long-lasting. Many children never recover from abuse, which causes multiple inward problems and complicated personality disorders. It was a miracle that I survived all these and functioned normally.

Dad's new marriage blessed us with two sisters, Helena and Bridie, who shared our lives. But when I was six years old, my Dad was hit with another curse. All his cattle contracted a disease and died. Since farming was his only livelihood, he had no choice but to emigrate to England to secure employment to provide for our needs. It was another emotional disturbance in my childhood, and I looked on it as abandonment.

I never saw my father again until I was 22 years old. I was very angry most of my life about being robbed of the love of a mother and a father in my childhood.

World War II broke out when I was nine. Since all food was rationed and there was no Daddy to sow vegetation on the farm, we experienced very lean years. We had to totally depend on my Dad's weekly check and on the goodness of the neighbors.

My maternal grandmother lived a few farms away. I experienced a lot of rejection from her also. I'm not sure if she was angry at my Dad for remarrying or if she was angry because my mother (her daughter) died at such a young age (22). Whatever her reason, she never had love to share with me.

When I was about eight years old, her daughter, who was my godmother, was getting married. In those days they had big country house weddings, which were very special. I had never been to one, but I sure looked forward to this one. When I had not received the invitation the evening before, I thought maybe I did not need one. But when I walked up to her house to ask what time I should come for the wedding, I will never forget the expression of rejection on my grandmother's face as she replied, "With those old raggedy clothes and no shoes and your hair all chopped up, don't you dare come near this place tomorrow to shame me." I cried all the way home. There was nowhere I could borrow a dress, or perhaps I was too humiliated to ask anyone.

I could not understand all the rejection of a little orphan girl. I had no one in my life who cared about my emotions. Talk about a barefooted loveless orphan. I've been there.

My brother John did not seem to be rejected as much as I was; both my stepmother and my grandmother loved him. I always thought it was because he was the only boy in the family. Or because he had bronchitis and Granny always catered to his chest with a healing cloth of red flannel, which was an Irish healing method. Today, as

I look back on the circumstances, I know John did not suffer from the spirit of rejection like I did. He was accepted.

Every year when Christmas Eve came, we'd hang up our stockings like all the kids in the neighborhood did. But the stockings were just as empty in the morning. When I'd go back to school after the Christmas holidays, all the children would be talking about the toys Santa brought them. I wondered why he didn't come to our house. Actually, we were lucky to have something to eat.

I struggled through my childhood till I finished parochial school. There was no high school in those days. It was only for rich kids who could afford to go to boarding school. We lived in what the Yanks would call the boondocks. Even if we had had a high school, there was no money for books, clothing or transportation.

After the war God sent us an American cousin, John Carney. He was my brother's namesake, an American soldier, who was on his way home from Germany where he had been with the U.S. Army. He had a desire to visit his ancestral home before returning to the States. He asked me what my goals were after school. There were no jobs in Ireland and no emigration to England until you were 18. The port of emigration to the States had been closed during the war, but now it was going to open again. I told him that I'd love to come to America, which had been my dream since I was a little girl. He responded very positively and promised that he would speak to his father about sponsoring me.

Would you believe it, he kept his promise! His father, who was my Dad's brother, had not communicated with us for years. But when I was 17, he sent me the necessary documents and a ticket. I was on board the *Mauretania* for my 18th birthday. I sailed from Cork harbor on May 19, 1948, full of hope for a successful future, leaving my rejected life behind, as I thought. I was now ready to explore freedom for the rest of my life.

When I arrived in New Jersey, I found that the job market for someone without a high school diploma was not very open. It was another rejection with which to start my new life.

Every American of my age had already graduated from high school, which secured them with a diploma. My aunts decided that I should do domestic work like they did when they emigrated. I heard their emigration story and the rejection they faced because they lacked an educational background. They had to do slave labor as domestics.

I agreed to this slave labor for a few years, till I got all my debts paid. During that time I would take a bus ride to New York City on my days off to visit girls from home and from the ship. They were all working as waitresses in Schraft's chain of restaurants. In no time at all I moved to the Big Apple and joined them.

My First Trip Back to Ireland

In May 1952, I made my first trip back to Ireland and met my Dad for the first time since I was seven years old. He was still working in England and John and my sister Helena had joined him. I made my first visit to England to see them.

I barely had time to get acquainted with my Dad when I had to return to the States. I saw how conditions were in England. There was still not much progress after the war. John and Helena thought I was more prosperous than they were and showed an interest in emigrating to the States. My other sister Bridie was still home on the farm with my stepmother, and she also expressed an interest in coming to the States.

After I returned from my vacation, I prepared the papers to bring Bridie first and secured her with employment. Eight months later I sponsored John and Helena. Now we were all together again in the land of our adoption. We had freedom, security, employment and potential for a great future as we all chose to make America our home. All four of us shared the same apartment for a few years, until our separate lives began to unfold.

John was drafted into the U.S. Army and I got married on May 19, 1956, to a staunch Irish man whom I loved. But the spirit of rejection hit again and destroyed our marriage relationship. The enemy was out to get me in every area of my life.

Five months after my wedding, my Dad passed away very suddenly, at the age of 57. I was saddened because I had just found out I was carrying his first grandchild. I had been looking forward to inviting him for his first visit to my home and to America.

Our old homestead 1940. Cloontumper house where we were all born & raised. Left to right are: Mary (10) Bridie (5) Helena (6) John(9)

Chapter 11

Sharing My Testimony

Revelation 12:11a (NIV)

They overcame him by the blood of the Lamb and by the word of their testimony.

Sharing my testimony became a way of life for me after I understood the scripture just quoted. Previously, I used to think, "Who cares about my story?" I thought no one else in the world had a rejected life like mine. Besides, it was not a life I was proud of, and I would rather cover it up and hide it than share it. It had never occurred to me that my life had value to God. Now no one can ever make me feel inferior or unloved again. Everybody is a real somebody in God's eyes. I am living proof that a person created in God's likeness can be restored to a productive life. God's seeds grow great crops.

After I returned from a missionary tour to China, Thailand and Taiwan with Nora Lam, where I shared my testimony in the underground church, God opened the door for me to share about the mission to China on Christian TV. A video of the crusade was going to run first, to explain the ministry, and then I was supposed to answer questions on what I experienced there and advertise Nora's upcoming banquet in Miami, of which I was chairperson. Shortly before the show began, they discovered that they had been sent the wrong video from California. But I still had to go on for 40 minutes, which gave me a chance to share my testimony. I knew that had to be an act of God, for I probably would never have had the opportunity to share my testimony on national television otherwise.

Since that time I have been sharing my testimony all over Florida, across the nation and Canada, and in the islands of Bermuda, Nassau, Jamaica, Cayman B.W.I. and the Virgin Islands.

The Lord has anointed my testimony to heal the hurts of the downtrodden and broken women. My ministry of inner healing for the rejected and hurting has touched the hearts of many divorced women who can't seem to make it after a crisis in their lives. My story of recovery gives them strength to be overcomers, to pick up the pieces and to move on to victory.

Some women, plagued by inner fears and guilts, poison their own systems and engender deterioration within themselves. They permit their lives to be eroded by the trauma and chemical poison of hatred, vengeance and unforgiveness for their former spouses. The Lord reminds us, "Vengeance is Mine, I will repay" (Rom. 12:19).

I am so happy that God blessed me with the gift of forgiveness. I know that if I had not forgiven all my loved ones who rejected me, my life would have degenerated and crumbled. Most talented women allow their lives to be wasted because of unforgiveness. They then wonder why their lives are fruitless.

If I had experienced a lot of love in my rejected life, I would never have found Jesus' love. I would not have had any need to look for it and I would not have recognized it if it came my way.

A few months ago my cousin Maureen celebrated her 25th wedding anniversary, which entailed a large family gathering, with relatives coming from out of state and from our homeland. During the course of the celebration, one of the guests said to me, "Mary, don't you feel sad participating in this type of party when your own marriage is long dead?"

I had to be honest and express the seed of truth in my answer. Seeing a marriage still alive after 25 years in this society is a blessing. Yes, I observed the excitement of the party that night and I saw my cousin full of joy and cheer as she greeted all her guests and danced the night away. She still has her lovely husband to love her and to provide a retirement for her. She still has two lovely sons and a beautiful home with all its glitter, Waterford crystal, china and valuable paintings—all the desires of her heart—but I would not exchange with her what the Lord has blessed me with.

God loves me too much to see me perish. Now I have freedom to become all that He has in mind for me. I know my new-found life has divine purpose. God's foundation stones, which are built into my spirit, guarantee me a rich harvest of His abundant love. No crime can be punished twice. No debt can be paid twice. He acted on my behalf.

Women's search for God is reflected in their cries for freedom, to be set free. My greatest hunger in my Christian walk is to bring *hope* to the rejected woman. My contribution is to gift them with a testimony of courage and truth.

My past was my teacher. Only, the knowledge I gained from it, I held onto. Failure is never final; we can decide to be a chooser, not a loser.

I believe God had a purpose for us hurting women when He raised up Women's Ministry Fellowships. He knew in these last days that so many of us would need healing and restoration. They have been a great blessing to me to share God's provision in my life. Last year at one of the International Conferences, I fellowshipped with women from all walks of life whom I had personally met as I ministered in their city or island. It was like having one large family of sisters. Many of them booked me for a meeting to share in their cities. The Lord has shown me that my ministry will take me into the most beautiful parts of the world to touch His women.

My life's purpose is people, and I know God is at work in me as a woman reaching people through His hands, through His life and through His love. I never thought of myself as His messenger. I am His hands, His feet and His mouthpiece. And I had to adjust my attitude to accept God's inventory of the treasures, the talents, the skills and the abilities He assigned to me at the moment of my conception.

When I became a partner with God, I began to discover and experience the abundant blessings He had planned for my life. Now I see Him alive and at work in my meetings; He had promised that signs and wonders would follow those who believe (Mark 16:17).

As I continue to touch women around the world, I go only where the Lord Jesus can accompany me and where I know He is welcome. He desired my companionship enough to die for me so He could redeem me back into His fellowship. Then my rejected life became a ministry of rewarding service to other women.

Our rejected lives can produce fruit. Women need to know that Jesus is alive and real. We are not wounded anymore; we're going on and striving for the high calling of God. No matter what the persecution, we must get out of our boats, out of deep water, and come ashore. God is in the restoration business.

Chapter 12

My Seven Years with Ruth Sweeney

II Chronicles 1:12

*Wisdom and knowledge is granted unto thee;
and I will give thee riches, and wealth, and
honour, such as none of the kings have had
that have been before thee, neither shall there
any after thee have the like.*

When I returned to Florida in 1985, I took a job as
a companion to Ruth Sweeney, a widow, aged 84, who
lived alone at Park Layne Towers in Hallandale. Her

third husband had gone home to the Lord. She was in poor state after a hip surgery. Her nurse Betty wanted time off to go up north and asked me to relieve her for a month. That month has lasted for seven years, as Betty became seriously ill and then passed away.

Ruth had had a serious drinking problem for many years. I prayed for her deliverance and the Lord healed her in 30 days. She also had a fear of water; she had not taken a shower for 26 years. After I prayed for her healing, she began taking regular showers. She also ate a box of chocolates a day, so I prayed over her and she got healed of that. She had diabetes as well, and I prayed over her and the Lord took it away. I didn't know she was healed of diabetes till I changed doctors a year later. He took blood tests and said, "Who said she has diabetes?" He took her off the medication that she had been on for years. Then, also, she would keep asking for ice cream cones all day long, and the Lord took that away too.

I watched the Lord do a miracle in her life in her old age. I was happy that He gave me compassion for her. It was so rewarding to watch her mind being renewed and coming alive. She began to read the Word daily and watch Christian TV.

Her renewed life became a challenge. She began to write letters to her relatives, started to read more and went to her doctor's appointments regularly without any rebellion.

After the miracle in her life unfolded, she allowed me to work on her home. Her condo had two bedrooms and two baths.

I replaced old furnishings and rugs and had some wall papering and decorating done. After I had it all fixed up comfortably, I felt the Lord telling me I would stay there for a season. With Ruth being 84, I felt it would be a short season.

It was beyond my wildest dreams that she would live through her 90th birthday and, at this writing, be close to her 91st.

After I was with her for four years, she asked me to make a commitment to remain with her while she lived, which I did. The Lord even laid it on her heart to bless me with an inheritance so I could retire when she passes on. I was not comfortable with this arrangement until her brother-in-law, who takes care of her finances, agreed with it. He came in from out of state to help her update her will. He was very pleased with the way I was caring for her and was assured that she was in secure hands.

That was not the only reason I stayed with her. We had become greatly attached to each other. Since she never had a daughter and I never had a mother, we became the perfect mother and daughter team. We found joy and happiness in each other. We never had a personality clash. Her home became my home. It was a place for me to rest in the Lord and study His Word.

I was able to accomplish many projects in my spare time. I took a course in computers and learned how to use a word processor. Then I purchased a word processor which gave me a lot of pleasure in practicing on it while I was preparing this book.

My life with Ruth is coming to an end. She is now bedridden and very frail and weak. She has lost a lot of weight too, but she doesn't have a pain or an ache. Her body is just deteriorating from old age. Her brother, who was ten years younger, passed away last year. Her sister also had passed away about a year after I came to Ruth. Now she is the only surviving member of her family. She calls me the daughter she never had. I hope she lives till my book is published, as I have been sharing it with her.

My seven years here in Hallandale, Florida, have been a time of great spiritual growth, a time of becoming. I became acquainted with the Word and the Spirit in a mighty way. I lived near TBN, where I volunteered to help on the prayer line of Christian TV. My previous seven years of traveling were an adventure! These seven years were a growth experience. I became a consistent reader and found a wealth of knowledge in Christian books and tapes and 24-hour Christian TV. God has blessed my time with Ruth as I served Him.

Chapter 13

God Multiplied My Loss into Something Greater: Financially, Spiritually, Physically and Emotionally

When my time with Ruth ends, I know God has a plan for me to serve Him somewhere else for the rest of my life. That's why He provided a retirement plan for me. After reading my story, you are aware that I started out with nothing—no alimony, no support of any kind. When I was divorced, all I could think of was working for the rest of my life, even into my old age.

My marital home, the one I was thrown out of, was finally sold last year. When my ex-husband remarried, I took him to court to force the sale. Would you believe it, the courts closed all the doors in my face? They said that my statute of limitations was up; that I should have put in this claim ten years sooner, when my son was 18. It was another attack of satan's rejection.

The judge didn't know that I knew God. After much intercessory prayer and three years of battle, I was in a service one night when a prophecy came forth for a Mary who was going through a lot of persecution from her ex-husband over property. In a service of about 3,000 people, I knew there had to be several hundred Mary's, but I stood up and claimed it. I couldn't believe that I was the only one who stood. He called me down to the front to pray over me and broke the curse. A few weeks later the house was sold.

I claimed Joel 2:25-26.

And I will restore to you the years that the locust hath eaten.... And ye shall eat in plenty, and be satisfied, and praise the name of the Lord your God, that hath dealt wondrously with you: and My people shall never be ashamed.

If our house had been sold and divided when I got divorced, my share would have been about $8,000 because it was only worth $50,000 and had a big mortgage. Thirteen years down the road it was sold for $220,000 and had only a $3,000 mortgage on it. The Lord protected my interest in it and I received my 50 percent of it. God sure is in the restoration business. What the devil meant for evil God meant for good.

Jesus died and bore all the legal judgment that was against me. He came on a love mission to show me God's original dream for me and forgiveness was the key I found to restoration. After I surrendered to the power of forgiveness, I reaped a harvest of full restoration, like Job, far beyond what I lost.

We can rob man and fool man all of the time, but we can never fool God. He is always awake and in control of every situation.

Tithing Became a Way of Life

After I read a book called *The Miracle of Seed Faith,* I wondered about all those testimonies, if they were real, and I decided to try it. Watching the 700 Club telethon one day, I pledged $100. I had read in the book that the seed would be multiplied a hundredfold. I had just opened a new checking account. That first month there was a $10,000 computer error in my account. I took no notice of it since I knew it was an error and they would have it taken out next month.

However, next month came and it was still there. I called the bank and they checked it out. The next day they called me back to tell me that the computer said I had made this deposit on such and such a date and the money was mine. I said, "That will be the day that I will have that kind of money, make that big of a deposit and forget that I made it."

The man continued to tell me that the law is, in the state of California, that if no one claims the money within six months, I get to keep it. I said, "Sure, that would never happen to me," but praise God it did. I left the money there for 13 months and no one claimed it. I prayed about it, and the Lord showed me that He wanted me to have a good car on the road. My old car, the one I drove across country in, had 96,000 miles on it. He knew it would not make it back east and that I was not safe in it. I went to the Ford dealer and bought myself a brand new LTD. The dealer kept trying to suggest every kind of finance plan for me, but I kept telling him I was going to pay cash. He must have thought I did not look like a woman who had all that cash.

After that, tithing became a way of life for me. I could testify of many other miracles that occurred since I became a tither. If you are not tithing, you are robbing yourself of so many blessings.

God provided a better retirement for me than if I had a husband to provide for me. He became my husband and provider.

Besides all the provision the Lord has accumulated for me, I have also reached Social Security benefits this year. He has shown me that He has provided for my retirement, and it's much better than that of women who have husbands to provide security for them. Yes, I have come a long way since that day I walked out of the courtroom stripped to the bone. Yet it is only through His provision.

I felt the Lord calling me into Rhema Bible College to study His Word for the mission He has planned for me. But in order to attend college, it is necessary to have a high school diploma, which I never had. I studied the GED program in Hallandale's adult night school and fulfilled Second Timothy 2:15: "Study to shew thyself approved...." At age 58, I graduated. Ruth Sweeney was then 88, and she came to my graduation exercise. She was just as proud of me as if I were her daughter; she made my night. *"All things are possible to those who believe!"* (See Mark 9:23.) We are never too old to become a high school graduate!

I have just applied to the Rhema Bible Training Center in Perth, Australia, for the next term, starting February 3, 1993. The mission field is wide open there. Women's Ministries is growing throughout Australia. It's a whole new world to explore and Jesus people are everywhere. Who knows where else God will open doors for one of His royal daughters who choose to follow Him. No good thing will He withhold from any woman who walks uprightly before Him (Ps. 84:11).

As you read this book, you will never be the same woman again. It is planting good seed in the fertile soil of your rejected life. Jesus said, "I have come, so that women may have life, and that they may live in abundance." (See John 10:10.) Instead of shame and dishonor, women will have a double portion of prosperity and everlasting joy.

As a former rejected woman, I am through with failure, mediocrity, sickness and poverty. God never planned for any of us to live with that. We can decide to take an oath of prosperity instead. As a woman, I vow to remember that the Lord is my shepherd, I shall not want; my cup runs over (Ps. 23).

If you have been blind to your value or to the possibilities around you, I want to open your eyes to see a dozen solutions to problems you thought were insurmountable. Perhaps you missed the answer in life. You may have been demoralized until you withdrew in surrender, in submission and in humiliation. Jesus will cause you to succeed where you failed and cause you to walk with dignity in this life because you are His daughter.

Since you are part of His Body, He wants to express Himself and carry out His mission of love to others through you as a woman. Practice letting Him do it. You see, He has no help but ours to bring in the lost. He has no tongue but ours to tell the world who He is. He has no hands but ours to do His work. He uses our feet to walk on holy ground. We are precious jewels to Him. So discover your roots in Him, and you will find a gold mine of divine riches for yourself and for the rejected women of our world.

SUNDAY, JUNE 18, 1989   The Miami Herald

Immigrant reaches goal at last

By KIMBERLY CROCKETT
Herald Staff Writer

HALLANDALE — With an eighth-grade education and dreams of living in "the land of opportunity," Mary Cunnane boarded a ship in Ireland and immigrated to the United States.

The year was 1948.

Forty-one years later, Cunnane says the land of opportunity has borne fruit. She received her high school diploma Friday from the Hallandale Adult Center.

"I get teary-eyed just thinking about it," she said. "The thought was in the back of my mind that I had missed something. Now I feel at 59 I have just begun."

World War II forced her to drop out of school in her native Ireland. While the country was spared from fighting, the war caused rationing of gasoline and rubber for bicycle tires, Cunnane lived on a small farm in County Mayo in northwest Ireland. She said she had no transportation to the high school four miles away.

After the war, Cunnane joined the mass of immigrants going to America. An uncle in New York sponsored her passage.

Her first job was as a waitress "in a restaurant which had a big population of Irish girls, and I felt right at home there."

She always thought she'd get a better job. But, without a high

ANTONIO OLMOS / Miami Herald Staff

DREAM FULFILLED: In her commencement attire, Irish immigrant Mary Cunnane, 58, of Hallandale.

school diploma, her opportunities were limited, she said.

Like many women of that era, Cunnane soon married and had children.

Cunnane said although she encouraged her three children to get a good education, it wasn't until she became a Christian in 1978 and wanted to go to Bible college that she thought of returning to school.

Now divorced, with grandchildren, Cunnane decided it was time to begin a new future for herself.

Cunnane moved to Hallandale in

1985 because she liked the tropical climate and because Florida is part of the "Bible belt."

With Bible college beckoning, Cunnane entered Hallandale's adult education program two years ago. She says she never got discouraged, not even when she failed her first test.

"The teachers at Hallandale Adult have been so kind and encouraging," she said. "They mother you and father you through the whole thing."

Chapter 14

God Did Not Show Me the Victory Till I Knew It Was Him

After I surrendered to the power of forgiveness, I reaped a harvest of full restoration above and beyond what I lost. I found a future full of *hope* for the rejected woman.

With the previous 13 chapters, I have brought you through my life of rejection and my life of restoration. You have felt the pain of my loveless childhood, the abandonment of my Daddy, my ex-husband and family. You saw my torn, scarred, broken, painful life and the final crushing blow of divorce, which left me emotionally wounded, homeless and alone.

As He rescued and sanctified me through all my suffering from a barefooted orphan to a divorced, homeless woman lost on America's highways, I claimed the promise in Romans 8:18: "I consider that our present sufferings are not worth comparing with the glory that will be revealed in us."

I have brought you through my years of darkness. But at age 48, I finally struck a match and the light came on in my life. Isn't it miraculous, what God can do with a broken life? Picture how He put all the pieces of broken pottery in my life back together again and restored me to wholeness.

I hope you will choose to rebuild your life because God has great plans for the rejected woman. Don't settle for the darkness; don't settle for anything less than God's best. Through my suffering I have gained a new understanding and caring concern for rejected and hurting women. The Lord has anointed my speaking ministry; my heart is so touched that He chooses to work through me to heal those women.

When you finish this book, I don't want you to remember Mary Cunnane's suffering. Rather, remember the miracle of restoration and healing that God did in my life. So don't look at yourself as a human failure. Christ died for your rejected life also. There is a price to be paid for salvation, but He already paid it for you at Calvary.

Forgiveness Is the Key

I have stressed the importance of forgiveness. I wish all the people who rejected me in my childhood were alive today so I could personally forgive them as I forgave my ex-husband. If all of them had not come into my life, I would not have a testimony or even a story to write.

Every seed that God planted in my life, He watered and nourished so it would produce fruit in preparation for His purpose, at such a time as this. If you have been pulled up by the roots like I was and transplanted in pain as a lonely reject, don't be blinded by revenge, hatred and bitterness to the fact that your real enemy is not flesh and blood.

Don't blame your spouse for destroying you. If you do, you are giving a foothold to satan, who is out to destroy you. Begin to realize that satan is the prince of this world and he is out to kill, steal and destroy (John 10:10).

When your spouse creates a violent act against you and breaks his covenant vows, you must realize he is captive to satan's kingdom. He is not responsible for his human behavior. His sin is not your problem and you must not identify him as your enemy. Once I had realized this concept, I learned one of the most crucial elements of *forgiveness*. I gained a whole new insight into satan's plan to destroy my home and my marriage.

I knew I could not fight that battle in the flesh; I had to engage in spiritual warfare, which can only be fought in the battlefield of prayer. Ephesians 6:12 came alive to me. I now recognize from where the power of darkness and the forces of evil come.

Only through the power of Jesus Christ is it possible to start all over, to forgive and forget, to start a new life of victory. It is not true that life begins at "40", it begins at Calvary. It began for me when I met *Jesus* on that lonely highway. Now I have a future full of *hope*. I am living proof that there is *Hope for the Rejected Woman*.

How I Died to Self and Became Victorious in Spite of My Rejected Life

When I was sitting by the Sea of Gallilee in Israel after a time of fasting and prayer, the Lord reminded me that I was not only His recovered daughter, but that I was also His hands, His feet and His mouthpiece. As His representatives, we carry on the work He left here on earth. He can only work through a person as His Holy Spirit can only dwell in the spirit of man.

Proverbs 20:27

The spirit of man is the candle of the Lord, searching all the inward parts of the belly.

How blessed we are to be chosen of the Lord so He can work His miracles through us. We must decrease so He can increase in us.

After I finished my tour of the 50 states, I was seeking a quiet place to settle down and write my book about all my travels and share what I found on America's highways and byways.

I returned to Florida in October '85. After I had written several chapters, I got bored. The motivation diminished, but my strong desire to be an author was still there. I had to seek God to find out why I felt like that. After much prayer and fasting, He awoke me from my sleep one night with this message: "Mary! When you decide to put more of Me in your book and less of yourself, I will inspire you to go on." I got the message loud and clear. I knew I had to die to my flesh. I realized I was writing a book about the great heroine I was, travelling through all the 50 states. I was taking all the credit and giving Him no glory.

I had to do some soul-searching and prepare myself to write God's book, *not mine*. I put the manuscript in the bottom drawer for a few years till the Lord gave me the inspiration to write about

His provision in my life. I had my own title for the book: *I Never Drive Alone.* But again He spoke to me in a dream and gave me the name for His book: *Hope for the Rejected Woman.* I woke up, put on the light and wrote it down. When I awoke next morning and read it over and over, I knew this book was birthed. I went through my notes from a Writer's Workshop. I recognized that the theme of my story was rejection because that's what I was healed from. It was like finding the root of a tree.

Chapter 15

My Lovely Brother John Was Called Home To the Lord

When I began to write this book, it was farthest from my thoughts that I would be concluding it with this chapter, sharing with you that my lovely brother John Carney was called suddenly out of my life. I am not sure if the Lord is trying to show me something in this. I mean the death of my mother when I was an infant, the death of my Dad when I was ready to be a mother, the death of my marriage and now the death of my only brother on May 19, 1992. This date now has three anniversaries in my life: the date I emigrated to the United States, the date of my marriage and now the date of John's death.

I know the Lord must want me to share this experience as part of my testimony. John's salvation, illness and death was one of the greatest spiritual experiences for which God ever prepared me. I look back on it with utmost delight and a sense of triumph. More light was shed on the mystery of John's salvation, which was predestined by the Lord. Here again my favorite scripture came to life.

For years after I got saved, I had been claiming Acts 16:31 for salvation for all my loved ones. John was heavy on my heart as I knew one day I'd meet the mother we never knew in Heaven. I had visions of her asking me, "Where is your baby brother? Why didn't you pray him into the Kingdom? Why didn't you minister the salvation message to him? Where is he?" The truth is, I did explain it to him on one of his visits to Florida, where he visited me every year. He had been really excited about it and made a commitment to receive Jesus as his personal Lord and Savior (John 3:3). When he went back home to Las Vegas, the enemy robbed him of the seed that had been newly planted in his life. He excitedly shared his experience with a friend, who discouraged him. But God showed me the difference between victory and defeat, and I knew He would turn it around.

The following winter when John came back to Florida, he rebelled at my Christian walk and refused to hear anymore about salvation. I said, "John, I love you and I want to see you in the Kingdom of God." He replied, "You will, Mary, and I will be there before you." He was right. He is gone on before me. Praise God.

On the last Sunday John spent with me in Florida, eight months before he became ill, we were invited to a friend's house for lunch after church. It was there that we met Paul O'Higgins, a native of Limerick, Ireland. God blessed Paul with a healing ministry. He and John got into a conversation about salvation and seemingly Paul explained it to him in such a way that John rededicated his life and not only did he receive salvation, he also received the baptism of the Holy Spirit. I am so happy that someone took this picture of Paul ministering to John. It must be meant for this chapter.

When John became ill, I flew to his bedside, in Las Vegas, to make sure satan had not robbed him again of the seed of eternal life. I led him in prayer and again he rededicated his life, forgave all his enemies and repented of his rebellion and his rejection of the most valuable gift that God provided for us through the death of His Son, our Savior, Jesus Christ.

Since all our family and friends lived in New York, I flew John into New York for his surgery.

Two days later he bravely faced the operating room. I went in again early that morning to lead him in prayer, to make sure he was really prepared to meet his Savior.

The results of his surgery were not good. The surgeon gave me the shocking news that the brain tumor was malignant and that John's life span was only six months longer.

In times such as these, even with all the human support available, the only sufficiency to be found is in God. John had given me "power of attorney" to handle all his finances and to make all the decisions for his provision for the months ahead. God entered my dilemma and gave me the assurance I needed. I also had to depend totally on His Word. I searched the Scriptures for strength and encouragement and I found in First Samuel 30:6 that David encouraged himself in God.

Shortly after John went through radiation therapy, he lost his speech and the power of his right hand. This was the hardest part of his rehabilitation. He could no longer communicate with us. I knew this loss was not of God, but He used it to minister to John's spirit. I gave John a mini-Bible and he was able to read God's Word. When I played Christian tapes for him, the anointed words of the songs witnessed to him. God's people came to pray with him and give him

Communion. He was always surrounded by happy people who loved and cared for him.

He spent his last three weeks in the Calvary Hospital for terminally ill cancer patients. I really appreciate those people who let him taste Heaven before he left us.

The last six days of John's life, I was able to stay in the hospital with him. I experienced such loving care and concern from all the staff. It was a place of peace and love.

During those last days, visitors were coming in and out of the hospital. They would pass remarks like, "Mary, if you are so close to God, and He has given you a healing ministry, why don't you ask Him for a miracle for your brother?" I said, "John did receive a miracle. He received 'eternal life,' which is far more valuable than a physical miracle. To be absent from the body is to be present with the Lord."

Thirteen hours before John expired, his kidneys failed. Hour after hour I watched all the organs of his body break down. Before he took his last breath, with the presence of the Lord still in the room, I kept praying in the Spirit as I knew the manifestation of John's transition was about to take place any minute. Then a glorious heavenly light shone around him as he slipped away into eternity. I rejoiced with the angels of Heaven as I knew that lovely mother we had never known was waiting for this reunion.

I had no time to think of what my new life would be like without a brother. I could only dwell on the peace and joy John had entered into, in his new home, serving God day and night, with no more medication, no more thirst, no more pain, no more seizures or tumors. He had come out of the great tribulation. God had wiped away all tears from his eyes and led him to the fountain of living waters.

Revelation 7:9-11 came to life, for there before me on the bed was only the shell that had held John while he was on earth. I finally realized that he was no longer with me. As I lifted my hands in praise and thanksgiving to my God, He was also wiping away the tears from my eyes, assuring me that John was now set free and washed in His blood. Death was completely dissolved and swallowed up in victory (I Cor. 15:54). When suffering ends, Christ begins.

Isaiah 53:4-5

Surely He hath borne our griefs, and carried our sorrows: yet we did esteem Him stricken, smitten of God, and afflicted. But He was wounded for our transgressions, He was bruised for our iniquities: the chastisement of our peace was upon Him; and with His stripes we are healed.

There was no more need for grieving or sorrowing for John; his mission here was over. He has seen Jesus and he is living in the heavenly realm with Him forevermore, thanks to the gift of salvation which God provided for us through His Son.

What a blessed hope; no one ever told me that loosing a loved one to Jesus was so special. It is because it is the beginning of eternal life. How blessed we are that He chose us to be heirs of His Kingdom. I am so happy that God blessed me with this experience before I finished this book. Now I know the real meaning of salvation, since God provided the way for me to experience it firsthand.

Where do you stand in relation to the salvation of your loved ones and friends who resist the gift of eternal life? How long have you been sharing the salvation message with them without effect? Keep in mind that you can only plant the seed. The Holy Spirit will water it. Pray them in with love and compassion and God in His mercy will provide the way to dispatch His angels to rescue them from the stronghold of the enemy. Our mightiest weapon is prayer; God has given it to us to yield for the Kingdom's sake.

God has shown me through John's salvation that the meat of my ministry is the salvation of the lost. The harvest is ripe, but the laborers are few (Matt. 9:37).

Paul O' Higgins ministering the baptism of the Holy Spirit to John in Florida.

For more information about Mary Cunnane's speaking engagements, healing services and divorce workshops at singles retreats or to purchase bulk supplies of this book for your seminars or retreats, write to:

Mary Cunnane

With **God** all things are possible
Matthew 19:26

Mary Cunnane • The Meadowlark
564 E. Crooked Hill Rd. • Pearl River, NY 10965

Mary Cunnane
Phone: 914-735-0390
Fax: 914-620-0563
Email: alacoque@webtv.com net